Mapping the World

VOLUME 6

MAPPING FOR GOVERNMENTS

GROLIER
EDUCATIONAL

Published 2002 by Grolier Educational, Danbury, CT 06816

This edition published exclusively for the school and library market

Produced by Andromeda Oxford Limited
11–13 The Vineyard, Abingdon,
Oxon OX14 3PX, U.K.

Copyright © Andromeda Oxford Limited 2002

Contributors: *Peter Evea, Stella Douglas, Peter Elliot, David Fairbairn, Ian Falconer*

Project Consultant: *Dr. David Fairbairn, Lecturer in Geomatics, University of Newcastle-upon-Tyne, England*

Project Director: *Graham Bateman*
Managing Editor: *Shaun Barrington*
Design Manager: *Frankie Wood*
Editorial Assistant: *Marian Dreier*
Picture Researcher: *David Pratt*
Picture Manager: *Claire Turner*
Production: *Clive Sparling*
Index: *Janet Dudley*

Design and origination by Gecko

Printed in Hong Kong

Set ISBN 0-7172-5619-7

Library of Congress Cataloging-in-Publication Data

Mapping the world.
    p. cm.
Includes index.
Contents: v. 1. Ways of mapping the world --v. 2. Observation and measurement -- v. 3. Maps for travelers -- v. 4. Navigation -- v. 5. Mapping new lands -- v. 6. Mapping for governments -- v. 7. City maps -- v. 8. Mapping for today and tomorrow.
ISBN 0-7172-5619-7 (set : alk. paper)
    1. Cartography--Juvenile literature. [1. Cartogaphy. Maps.] I. Grolier Educational (Firm)

GA105.6 .M37 2002
562--dc21

        2001051229

Contents

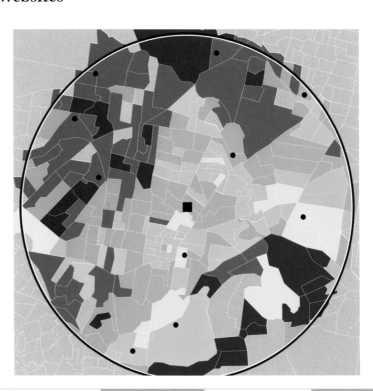

About This Set

Mapping the World is an eight-volume set that describes the history of cartography, discusses its importance in the development of different cultures, and explains how it is done. Cartography is the technique of compiling information for, and then drawing, maps or charts. Each volume examines a particular aspect of mapping and is illustrated by numerous artworks and photographs selected to help understanding of the sometimes complex themes.

After all, cartography is both a science and an art. It has existed since before words were written down and today uses the most up-to-date computer technology and imaging systems. It is vital to governments in peacetime and in wartime, as much as to the individual business person, geologist, vacationer−or pirate! Advances in mapmaking through history have been closely involved with wider advances in science and technology. It demands some understanding of math and at the same time an appreciation of visual creativity. Such a subject is bound to get a little complex at times!

What Is a Map?

We all think we know, but the word is surprisingly difficult to define. "A representation of the earth, or part of the earth, or another part of the universe−usually on a flat surface−that shows a group of features in terms of their relative size and position." But even this long-winded attempt is not the whole story: As explained in Volume 1, most early cultures tried to map the unseen−the underworld, the realms of gods, or the unknown structure of the cosmos. Maps are not just ink on paper or lines on a computer screen. They can be "mental maps." And the problem of mapping a round object−the earth or one of the planets−on a flat surface means that there is no perfect flat map, one that shows precise "size and position."

The cartographer has to compromise to show relative location, direction, and area in the best way

for a specific purpose. He or she must decide what information to include and what to leave out: A sea chart is very different from a subway map. This set explains how the information is gathered−by surveying, for example−and how the cartographer makes decisions about scale, map projection, symbols, and all other aspects of mapmaking.

Researching a Subject

Separate topics in the set are presented in sections of from two to six pages so that your understanding of the subject grows in a logical way. Words and phrases in *italic* are explained more fully in the glossaries. Each glossary is specific to one volume. There is a set index in each volume. Recommended further reading and websites are also listed in each volume. At the bottom of each left-hand page there are cross-references to other sections in the set that expand on some aspect of the subject under discussion.

By consulting the index and cross-references, you can follow a particular topic across the set volumes. Each volume takes a different approach. For example, different aspects of the work of the famous mapmaker Gerardus Mercator are discussed in several volumes: the mathematical basis of his map projection in Volume 2, his importance for navigation in Volume 4, and his success as a businessman in Volume 5.

The continuous effort to improve mapping is part of the history of exploration, navigation, warfare, politics, and technology. All of these subjects−and many more−are discussed in *Mapping the World*.

Maps and artworks help explain technical points in the text

Cross-references to other relevant sections in the set give section title, volume number, and page references

Introduction to Volume 6

Mapping is important for governments. It provides information about their peoples and lands, and helps them plan for the future. Every nation realizes that having good maps of its own area is essential. This volume examines how governments organize mapping programs and what features they map (such as the landscape, their people, and their natural resources). Maps also hold vital information for nations at war: Generals planning military campaigns use them, and so do soldiers on the battlefield. They are sometimes even used for propaganda purposes.

Aspects of the section subject are sometimes explained in separate information boxes

Summary introduces the section topic

Main entry heading to a two-, four-, or six-page section

Each volume is color-coded

Photographs and illustrations of people, locations, instruments—and, of course, maps—add to the text information

Calculating Longitude

For a long time sailors were able to work out their latitude, or position relative to the equator. While explorers kept in sight of the coast, there was little need to calculate how far they had traveled in an easterly or westerly direction. However, as explorers traveled further away from home, they needed more and more to know their longitude.

Lines of longitude, called *meridians*, are imaginary lines on the earth's surface running directly from the North Pole to the South Pole. Longitude is measured eastward and westward from the Prime Meridian (0°). In 1884 an international agreement fixed this line to run through Greenwich in London, England. The longitude of a point is the angle at the center of the earth between the meridian on which it lies and the Prime Meridian. The degrees are numbered west and east of Greenwich up to 180°. Establishing position in an east-west direction was

historically much more difficult than working out a ship's latitude, and for centuries sailors could do no more than estimate their longitude, often not very accurately, using dead reckoning (see page 11).

Early methods of trying to measure longitude involved noting the distances of certain stars from the moon or observing the orbits of Jupiter's moons, but none was accurate enough. It is possible to calculate longitude by using the position of the stars. However, the problem with this method is that the stars shift their position eastward every day. To use their positions to calculate your own position, you need to know the precise local time relative to a fixed reference point.

The earth turns 360° (a complete revolution) every day and 15° every hour. If a navigator knew the time in Greenwich, England, which is on the Prime Meridian, or 0° of longitude, and also knew the precise local time, it would be simple math to multiply the time difference (in hours) by 15 to give

John Harrison 1693-1776

In 1714 the British Board of Longitude announced a competition. Whoever could invent a method for accurately finding a ship's longitude would win a huge prize of £20,000. The government was not giving away such a large amount of money for nothing. Being able to calculate longitude could provide enormous advantages in international trading and military seapower, to say nothing of helping prevent disasters at sea resulting from poor navigation. To win the prize, the ship's longitude had to be measured to an accuracy of 0.5 degrees, or 30 minutes, of longitude. Harrison knew that he could win if he could produce a very accurate marine clock, or chronometer. His fourth, brilliant design proved to be accurate enough to win the competition. It was tested at sea during 1761 and 1762, and experiments found that over a 5-month period it had an error of just 1.25 minutes of longitude, easily accurate enough to win the prize.

◄▲ Harrison with an earlier clock (above) and the compact design of his fourth model (left).

the ship's longitude. To do this, there had to be an accurate way of measuring time.

Johan Werner first suggested using some sort of timekeeper as early as 1514 but was not able to build one that had enough accuracy. Until John Harrison's designs clocks had to be constantly adjusted. And the problem was even worse at sea, with changes in temperature, dampness, and the ship's movement all upsetting a clock's delicate mechanism. Harrison succeeded in overcoming all these problems. His development of the marine chronometer in the 18th century finally allowed navigators to accurately determine their longitude. By referring to nautical almanacs that were compiled by astronomical observatories, the navigators could work out their position east or west as well as north or south.

◄ World time zones. The time changes by one hour for every 15° of longitude traveled around the earth. You lose or gain a day crossing the International Date Line.

Time Zones

Because the earth spins by 15° of longitude every hour, anyone traveling in a westerly direction will lengthen the day by one hour for every 15° of longitude traveled. Similarly, traveling eastward will shorten the day by one hour. This distance is a long way at the equator, but less and less the further south or north you are. A sailor could not continue to gain or lose time for ever, so in 1884 a Canadian engineer called Sir Sandford Fleming suggested a system of time zones (see diagram on page 20). He also proposed the International Date Line. This line runs north-south through the Pacific Ocean and avoids major landmasses. When a traveler crosses the line going westward (say, flying from Los Angeles to Sydney), a day is added. Nine on the morning of June 10 immediately becomes 9 a.m. on June 11. In the opposite direction (for example, from Auckland in New Zealand to Honolulu) 9 a.m. on June 11 becomes 9 a.m. on June 10.

SEE ALSO: LATITUDE, LONGITUDE, AND POSITIONING **2:** 26-29; FINDING YOUR WAY ON THE OCEAN **4:** 10-11

20

21

Captions explain context of illustrations

Why Governments Need Maps

Maps are an important record of land ownership, establishing boundaries and other land rights, such as access to water. In the past rich and powerful landowners in Europe and in the Far East would have maps produced of their estates as a way of showing how important they were. Governments also found it useful to draw up maps of who owned what piece of land.

Many early maps in Europe were produced for rich and powerful people such as royalty and the owners of large areas of land. For example, a wealthy English landowner named Thomas Seckford paid for the estate surveyor Christopher Saxton to survey and map every county in England. In 1571 Saxton published his *Atlas of England and Wales*, which was not only the first atlas of the country but also the first national atlas anywhere in the world.

Other surveyors produced similar maps, but it was expensive to create, engrave, and print maps of this kind. Some mapmakers tried to raise money by advertising in local newspapers and circulating *prospectuses* among local landowners to persuade them to subscribe to the creation of a map. As a result the maps made tended to emphasize or even exaggerate the size of the estates of the landowners who paid for the work.

The Needs of War

Governments also needed accurate maps, but for different reasons—and they had the money to pay for them. The first motive was information for war. For instance, in 1746 the Scots, led by Bonnie Prince Charlie, rebelled against the British government. An army sent north against the rebels

ran into trouble because it had no good maps. So the British commissioned a Scot, William Roy, to make an accurate survey and map of Scotland.

In 1763 Roy proposed to the British governmment that he make a national map of the British Isles. But the idea was rejected because of cost, and he had to continue to map only castles, forts, and other defenses. The first national map did not become a reality until after 1791, when Britain was at war

▲ European monarchies wanted maps not just of their own lands but paid for other countries to be mapped as a way of advertising their own importance. This is the elaborate *cartouche* of a map of the Netherlands. Published in 1788 by the Académie Royale des Sciences in Paris, it was commissioned by the French king.

SEE ALSO: *CROSSING THE CONTINENTS* **5:** *24–27; CHINESE AND JAPANESE URBAN PLANS* **7:** *10–11*

with France, with the setting up of the Ordnance Survey mapping agency. It was called "Ordnance" because the surveyors came mainly from artillery regiments of the British army. (Ordnance is military supplies, particularly guns and ammunition.)

Mapping New Territory

In other countries governments began to realize the need for maps. In the U.S. after the Revolutionary War ended in 1783, both George Washington and Thomas Jefferson were eager to get surveys and maps of the territory to the west of the original 13 North American colonies. Thomas Jefferson became chairman of a committee set up by the new U.S. government to organize the settlement and subdivision of the new territory. This required *cadastral maps*. Cadastral maps, which register the

ownership of land, are essential to a government when it is setting taxes.

The United States Public Land Survey System mapped an enormous area of land, more than 695 million square miles (1.8 billion square kilometers) to the west of the Appalachian Mountains. Most of the work was done in wild and difficult country by private contractors under the control of Thomas Hutchins, the federal Surveyor-General. They divided the land into townships, each one 6 square miles in area. It was this way of subdividing the land that led to the checkerboard patterns of the American landscape that can still be seen today.

▼ A 19th-century cadastral map of North Dakota, showing the straight lines of ranch divisions with the owners named within them. The state capital of Bismarck is in the south toward the center of the map.

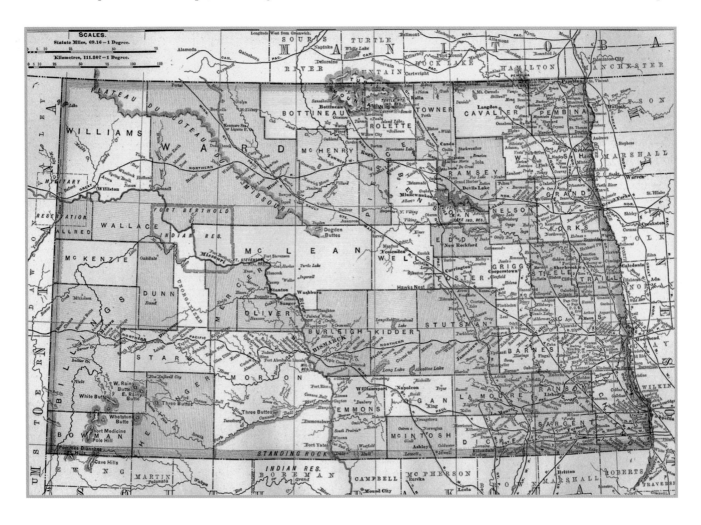

Governments Take Over Mapping

The needs of armed forces, as we have seen, were one reason why governments began to organize mapmaking from the late 17th century on, but it was not the only reason. Before then private mapmakers had tried to make a quick profit by copying other maps and getting information from travelers and explorers. More scientific methods were now known: They were more accurate, but much more expensive.

One way of making an accurate survey uses a process called triangulation. One side of a triangle is measured accurately, and then trigonometry is used to calculate the lengths of the other two sides of the triangle. In this way a whole country can be accurately measured by dividing it into triangles. This takes time and money to pay for scientific surveying teams. It is so expensive that usually only governments can afford to do it.

French Mapmakers

Triangulation and many other modern mapping techniques were first applied over a large area in France. Louis XIV was king of France from 1643 to 1715. His minister Jean-Baptiste Colbert persuaded him that good maps were essential if he was to rule France effectively. Between 1675 and 1685 Colbert organized the first true surveying and mapping of France by the *Académie des Sciences*. Much of this was done using triangulation.

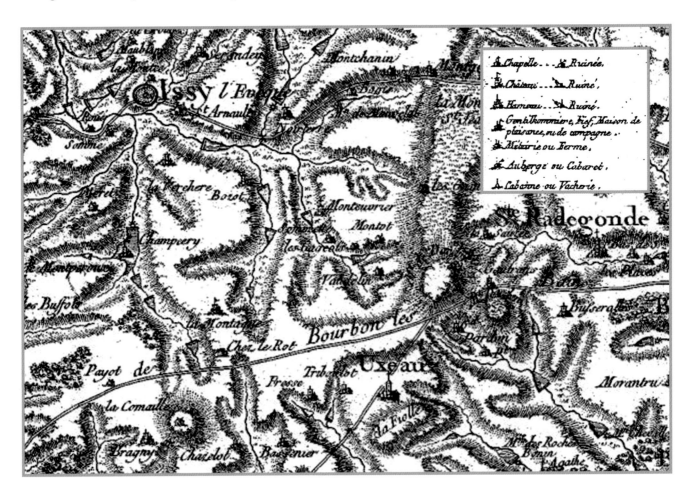

SEE ALSO: *HOW TO MAKE MEASUREMENTS FOR MAPS* **2:** *12–17*

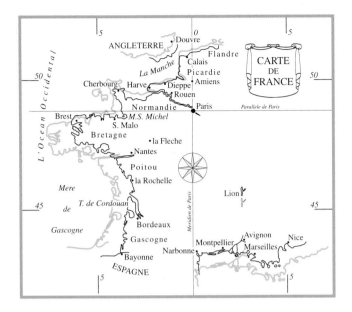

◄The map that made Louis XIV unhappy. It shows the old coastline and the newly drawn coastline, which made France smaller. The map is part of the *Carte de France Corrigée,* or "Corrected Map of France."

In 1684 a new map was produced showing the older outline of the French coast and the new outline drawn by more scientific methods. Louis XIV is reported to have been very unhappy with the new map because it showed France to be smaller than previously thought! He complained that his cartographers had lost him more land than any general, meaning that even wartime losses of territory could never be as big as the apparent loss of territory indicated by the new map. (France was almost constantly at war over territory during Louis XIV's reign.) No land had been actually lost, of course; the older maps were simply wrong.

Major contributions to the early mapping of France were made by the Cassini family. César-François Cassini (1714–1784), the third generation of the Cassini family to work for the French monarchy, was a French astronomer and cartographer who directed the work on a map of the whole of France.

It was commissioned and paid for by the next king of France, Louis XV, and surveying began in 1747. Its completion was delayed by the French Revolution of 1789. The revolutionary government that destroyed the French monarchy eventually published the map in 1815 with the title *Carte Géométrique de la France* (Geometric Map of France). It was the first map of an entire country drawn according to modern mapping principles. It consisted of a series of 182 sheets, mapping the country at a scale of 1:86,400.

Following France's Lead

Other national governments saw the advantages of the Cassini map, not just for military defensive advantage but also for civil planning, working out where to build roads and bridges, for example. Spain, Austria, and Britain were among the first countries to begin their own national surveys.

◄A Cassini map of the Dordogne area of France, part of the *Carte de France*, 1775. The map has a key showing castles and churches–including ruins–farms, and inns.

►A portrait of Jean-Dominique Cassini (1748–1845). He was an astronomer. Astronomical observers contributed ideas to early scientific mapping.

National Mapping Agencies

Around the world governments have set up national mapping agencies whose job it is to produce maps of their country. In Europe they were exclusively military to begin with, but then gradually became civilian. In the U.S. and Canada, where defense was not the first priority of the government, they were never military organizations.

The history of national mapping in many countries shows that the newest techniques of mapmaking have been developed by government agencies first. Nineteenth-century national mapping agency staff had access to brand new *theodolites* and other field survey equipment. Expensive field expeditions with many people employed in measuring were sent out into the new territories of western North America. Similar survey parties helped revise the maps of European nations and make new maps at ever-larger scales. The latest printing technology was installed in the agency head offices to produce high-quality maps on paper.

The setting up of national agencies happened at different times over a long period. For example, Japan set up the Imperial Land Survey in 1888; but countrywide government mapping of China did not start until the 1950s. In fact, most countries of the world had no government mapping agency until after World War II (1939–45).

If the maps were for military use, it was important, of course, to keep them secret! In the early 19th century most of the topographic maps produced by national mapping agencies were not sold to the general public: They were seen as official military documents. This view is still held by national mapping agencies in some countries.

The Ordnance Survey

In Great Britain the Ordnance Survey started to produce maps in order to defend the country against the threat of invasion. As mentioned on page 6, detailed maps of the south coast of Britain were produced in the early 19th century so that defenses could be strengthened against the French and army exercises could be carried out. In Britain maps are still produced by the Ordnance Survey.

The Ordnance Survey has been a wholly civilian organization since 1983. It produces more than a thousand different recreation and leisure maps a year, at a variety of scales showing all parts of the country, and sells them to the public. It is so important that around £100 billion worth of economic activity depends on its maps in some way, from building firms to haulage companies.

Its importance to the British government lies in the information it supplies to help decisions about the country's *infrastructure*. Where should industries be sited? Should permission be granted for the building of new houses in areas of countryside? What routes should new railroads take?

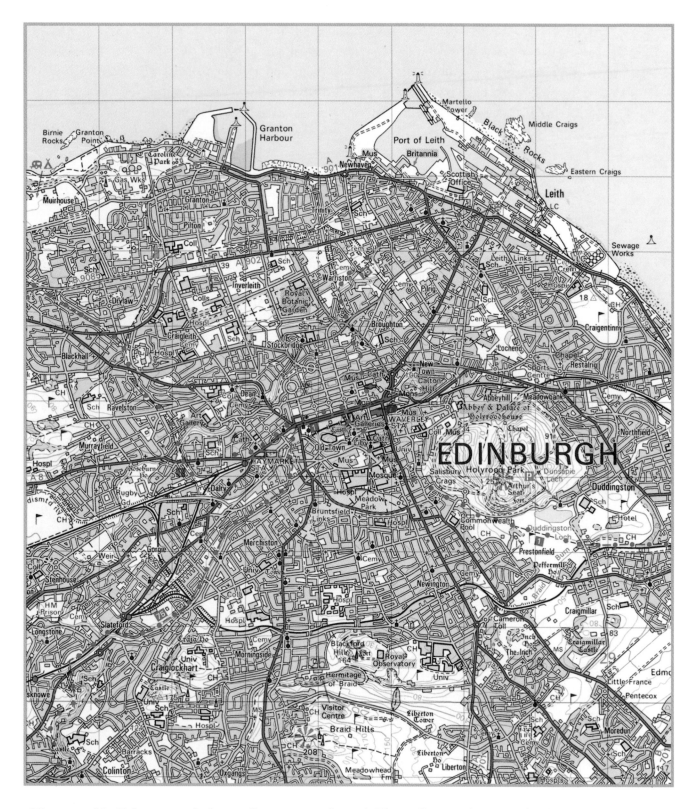

◀Compare this 19th-century Ordnance Survey map of Edinburgh, Scotland, with the modern version above. The most obvious difference is the lack of color. Printing processes could not yet produce all the shades.

▲ The earlier map is on a scale of one inch to one mile = 1:63,360, the modern map is 1:50,000. Red roads are main routes, yellow roads are fewer than 4 meters wide. Numbers in red boxes show national cycle routes.

North American Agencies

In the U.S. the United States Geological Survey (USGS) produces maps for the government, for publishers, and for the general public. The U.S. Public Land Survey that was set up in 1785 to help with registering land claims originally carried out this task. The USGS was established in 1879.

The USGS was founded to survey and map the new lands to the west of the original colonies. As its name suggests, it was also to map mineral and farming resources. High-quality topographic maps of the landscape helped in dividing up the land for incoming farmers and settlers. Mapping was also useful for constructing roads and railroads into the interior. Only in 1925 did the USGS start producing a topographical map of the entire U.S. The job was not finished until 1990. The work of the USGS has now expanded into many other areas. Its Biological Resources Division analyzes the U.S. ecosystem, for example. The USGS Topographic Section does the mapping.

In Canada the Center for Topographic Information, based in Ottawa, produces maps of the country. The first maps were drawn by the Geological Survey of Canada. Like the similar organization in the U.S., it was set up (in 1841) in order to find and map mineral resources such as coal, gold, and iron ore. The importance of these to Canada to this day can be seen by the fact that the Center for Topographic Information is part of a department called Natural Resources Canada.

War Improves Mapping Techniques

The biggest change in the work of national mapping agencies throughout the world happened in the 20th century after World War II. A report produced by the U.S. Air Force in 1940 stated that less than 10 percent of the world was mapped in enough detail even for simple pilot charts. During the war it became clear that making maps from aerial photographs was a quick and accurate way of creating map coverage over a large area. During war-

▲ A map of Philadelphia produced in 1898 by the USGS. The map shows the street layout and lowlying marshy areas in the southwest but does not show height or the *relief* of the land.

SEE ALSO: *NATIONAL ATLASES* **6**: *14–15; STORING IMAGE DATA IN GIS* **8**: *16–17*

time maps have to be made as quickly as an army moves position in attack or retreat. Using aerial photography, measurements of the landscape could be made quickly, and maps could be drawn from them immediately. The science of *photogrammetry* (making measurements from photographs) improved greatly from 1939 to 1945.

In peacetime national mapping agencies adopted the techniques of photogrammetry to improve and complete national mapping. In addition, large areas of the developing world were mapped using photogrammetric methods. Aerial photographs were taken of vast areas of Africa, Southeast Asia, the Caribbean, and the Middle East and maps produced.

Usually these maps were created by government mapping agencies of richer countries as a form of aid to poorer countries.

Changing from Military to Civilian Work

Today almost every country in the world has its own national mapping agency. Often agencies use private commercial companies to help with the official government work. In some countries the national mapping agency is still a military organization. In Australia, for example, the mapping agency AUSLIG produces its maps in a joint exercise with the army's Royal Australian Survey Corps. In 2001 AUSLIG began to loosen its ties to the military when it merged with another government agency that creates maps, called Geoscience Australia. There is a tendency for government mapping agencies to start as military organizations and then become civilian.

The main job of the national agency in some countries is to complete the national map. In others the task is to keep the existing maps up-to-date.

► A Canadian map. Like many mapping organizations, the Center for Topographic Information uses a grid system to divide up the country, with each square identified by a letter or number. People can get larger scale maps of any area by referring to the grid letters and numbers. The modern Ordnance Survey map on page 11 also has a grid system to help the reader find places or features.

◄ Today the USGS does much more than just mapping. USGS chief scientist Robert Wallace presents his ideas on earthquakes around the San Andreas Fault on the West Coast of the U.S. to other scientists.

National Atlases

Many countries have books that show, through maps, graphs, and tables, the geography of the country concerned. They are published by the government and are called national atlases. They show information not just about the physical geography of the country, such as its mountains and rivers, its soils and mineral deposits, and so on, but also the country's human geography, showing where people live, transportation systems, and details of the country's economy.

Atlases are named after a figure in ancient Greek mythology. Atlas was a god who rebelled against the ruler of the gods, Zeus, and was punished by being made to hold up the heavens on his back for all time. The 16th-century cartographer Gerardus Mercator began the tradition of using an image of the mighty Atlas on the first page of map books. These books then became known as atlases.

In 1970 the first national atlas of the U.S. was published. It consisted of a 400-page book of maps that gave information about the human and physical geography of the U.S. It cost more than $100 and so was usually found only in the libraries of schools, colleges, and universities. The Library of Congress has digitized and republished the maps from the 1970 National Atlas, and it is now available through their website: www.loc.gov.

In 1997 the U.S. Geological Survey (USGS) and other partners, including CNN (Cable Network News), began developing a new National Atlas of the U.S. This atlas is intended to be a reference available to all computer users. It does not just consist of paper maps in a book but also offers on-line interactive maps for those who have access to the Internet at www.nationalatlas.gov. This enables people to print and query not just the maps but facts about all aspects of American life.

It includes information in the form of statistical data about volcanoes, soils, and rivers, and human information such as crime patterns, population distribution, and patterns of disease.

The information is gathered from all of the U.S. government's agencies, including the Census Bureau, the Department of the Interior, the Department of Agriculture, as well as the USGS. While information about mountains and rivers does not usually change, or at least changes very slowly, "human" mapping does, so the atlas will have to be updated again some time in the near future.

Other National Atlases

More than 80 countries of the world now have national atlases, including Vietnam, Taiwan, Peru, El Salvador, and Tanzania. Some of these nations have produced atlases not just to show information about their country and its boundaries but also as symbols of independence after being ruled as a colony by a foreign power.

The National Atlas of Canada has been in existence for a long time. Its first edition came out in 1906, and since then a total of five editions have been published. Like the U.S. atlas, it gives information about the people, the economy, and the physical geography of Canada. The fifth edition consists of 93 pages in both French and English versions. Again like the American National Atlas, the way the information is presented has also changed. Originally a book, it is now an interactive publication available on the World Wide Web. It can be found at http://atlas.gc.ca.

China too has a national atlas called the National Economic Atlas of China. It has more than 265 full-color maps showing all aspects of life in China. It details China's growth as a world economic power. After many years of secrecy and isolation China is now looking to promote trade with the West. This atlas symbolizes a new openness in its government.

Surprisingly few European countries have national atlases produced by national agencies. One of the few is Sweden, with a book and CD atlas.

SEE ALSO: MERCATOR AND ORTELIUS: TWO MAPPING MASTERS 5: 12–13; COLONIAL BIAS IN MAPPING 5: 36–37

uito Surveillance:
nulative Report

)ata from reports made
en 1 JAN 00 and 8 DEC 00.

Any Positive

Test Sample Submitted

No Reports

Not Participating

county and county
ent data are based on
ory tests of mosquitoes
ed by state or local
agencies. Mosquitoes
ted by species and
. Note that the map
es all areas of positive
med or probable)
ile virus results, but
cessarily all areas
bmitted samples
s with no reports.

: These data are provisional and
evised or adjusted in the future.

This map is available at: http://nationalatlas.gov/virusprint.html

◄ National atlases do not just show features like mountains and rivers, or manmade things like roads and cities. They can map aspects of the nation's life that may be of particular importance at a particular time. The 2000 U.S. National Atlas provided a visual record of the spread of West Nile Virus in the northeast of the country. The mosquito-borne virus had not been seen in the U.S. before 1999. The atlas showed not just where tests for infected mosquitoes had been carried out and where they were positive, but also vast areas in the south of the country where testing was going to take place (see map, below). The problem is that the disease is carried by birds that have been bitten by infected mosquitoes. These birds then migrate south in the winter, taking the disease with them.

veillance Area

)ata represents the program
g the Fall of the year 2000.

Participating

Not Participating

ap depicts the 22
ts of cooperative
ent funds for
ile virus (WNV)
ance to work with the
for Disease Control
vention, for the year
The recipients were
because they were
d by the WNV in 1999,
use they have a high
al for being affected
uture because of bird
on patterns. Maine,
ampshire, and
t joined the
n in September.

: These data are provisional and
vised or adjusted in the future.

This map is available at: http://nationalatlas.gov/virusprint.html

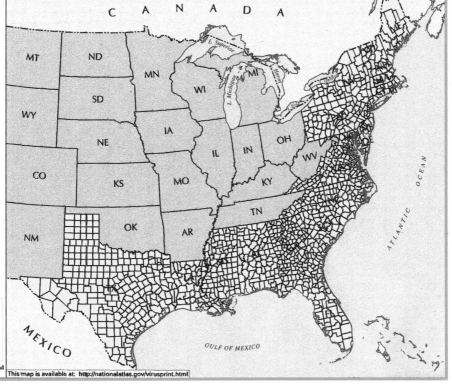

Mapping Features below the Surface

Governments need maps in peacetime for a number of reasons: to allocate new territories to settlers, to organize the collection of taxes, and to plan building work. There is another very important reason. The minerals in the ground are a vital source of a nation's wealth. Until the 19th century finding them was a matter of luck.

A person who studies rocks is called a geologist. Geologists use maps that are already in existence that show surface features of the landscape as a basis and draw details about the rocks on top of them. They find out about the rocks by noting where they appear on the surface (outcrops) and by examining mine shafts and quarries. Often they dig trenches, and they also drill through the surface.

Recently, new methods have been used such as *seismic surveys.* The shock waves from small detonations of explosives buried underground are recorded at the surface. Because these waves travel at different speeds through different rocks, geologists can map the underground features without digging or drilling. Ground-penetrating radar can be used to find the same information.

There are limits to geological mapping. An oil well can be as deep as 25,000 feet (7,600 m), too deep for seismic surveys, so the geological maps can only show that favorable rocks—sandstones and silt-stones—are present, not that the oil is actually there.

The history of Australia is an example of just how important such discoveries can be. Until the second half of the 20th century Australia was still mostly a farming country. When geological surveying and mapping improved, much of it done by government surveyors, massive mineral resources were found and exploited to transform Australia into a rich industrial nation. Australia has more iron ore than just about any country, plus large stores of natural gas, coal, oil, lead, zinc, silver, diamonds, and gold.

William Smith (1769–1839)

The Australian geological surveyors, and geologists throughout the world, were following the lead of one brilliant mapmaker. The first nationwide geological map was of England and Wales, produced by William Smith in 1815. It was of economic importance because it helped locate the coalfields that provided the energy for Britain's industries.

Unlike in most other countries, where much of the geological mapping would be done by govern-ment organizations, Smith produced this remarkable map on his own, working for more than 15 years.

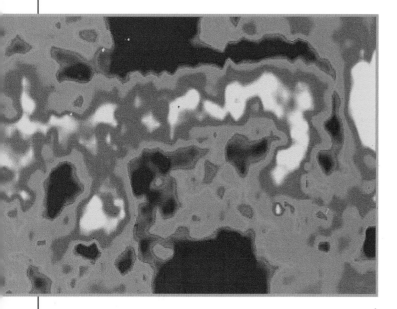

◀ A computer image of magnetic fields beneath the Effigy Mounds National Monument in Iowa. From this "instant map" archeologists can find areas of interest for further exploration.

▶ Smith's beautiful map uses different colors to show different rocks, like granite and coal. By following his methods, people could for the first time predict where oil, coal, even gold might lie.

STRATA
OF
ENGLAND AND WALES.
WITH PART OF
SCOTLAND;
EXHIBITING
THE COLLIERIES AND MINES.
THE MARSHES AND FEN LANDS ORIGINALLY OVERFLOWED BY THE SEA;
AND THE
VARIETIES OF SOIL
ACCORDING TO THE VARIATIONS IN THE SUBSTRATA,
ILLUSTRATED BY THE MOST DESCRIPTIVE NAMES
BY W. SMITH.

THE GERMAN OCEAN

IRISH SEA

THE

FIRTH OF CLYDE

FIRTH OF FORTH

St. GEORGE'S CHANNEL

CAERNARVON BAY

CARDIGAN BAY

BRISTOL CHANNEL

THE ENGLISH CHANNEL

EXPLANATION

Mapping People

Governments need to know about the people who live in their country. They require information such as how old the people are, the types of homes they live in, and where they work. They want this information to plan for the future and to know what services to provide, such as schools and hospitals.

They find this information through a census, which is a count of how many people there are in a country and what those people are like. From the census information maps can be drawn showing differences that exist between people in income, type of home, and level of education and health.

In the U.S. one of the reasons for the census is to support the democratic principle of one man, one vote. The number of people living in a state is used to calculate how many representatives each state is to have in Congress. The U.S. Census Bureau, which organizes the census in the U.S., completed its most recent one in March 2000.

The bureau presented the president with the population figures and maps of each state on January 1, 2001. From these figures on April 1 the states received information telling them how many representatives they could send to Congress.

The first census in the U.S. took place in 1790, when Thomas Jefferson used United States marshals to help him count a population of 4 million people. A census has taken place every 10 years since then. Each time the number of people and the amount of information collected has increased, and so in 1870 maps, charts, and diagrams

► A map of New York City showing where people of different ethnic backgrounds live. Such maps can help city planners–and they can also help politicians campaign to get elected!

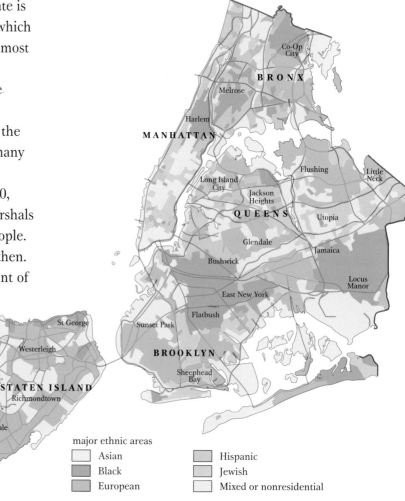

major ethnic areas

- Asian
- Black
- European
- Hispanic
- Jewish
- Mixed or nonresidential

SEE ALSO: *Maps of Invisible Things* **1**: *34–35*; *Applications of GIS* **8**: *12–15*

◀ A photograph of the Hollerith Tabulator, which used holes punched into cards as a way of processing the data collected in the 1890 U.S. Census. It meant that the census results were organized in record time.

were published to illustrate the most significant results. The amount of information became so great that for the 1890 census statistician Herman Hollerith (1860–1929) produced one of the first computers in the form of punched cards and an electric tabulating machine. He was the founder of International Business Machines (IBM).

The 2000 census in the U.S. was the largest ever. Most people filled out a form, which was sent to them by mail, but in remote places census enumerators visited people in their homes. Computers then analyzed the data. From the information the Census Bureau can produce maps showing details

about people throughout the country. This is called the Tiger Mapping Service, and through the Internet anyone can get access to this detailed information.

The Importance of Mapping the Census

The first modern Japanese census in 1920 showed that the population was 57 million. By 1940 it was 70 million. The most striking thing that the Japanese census has revealed since World War II is that the birthrate is one of the lowest in any country, and life expectancy is one of the highest. Information like this affects government planning. An aging population needs things like more hospitals.

But Japan consists of four main islands and many smaller ones. Where are the older people? Are they in Tokyo or on the smaller islands? A *demographic map* can help put the hospitals in the right place.

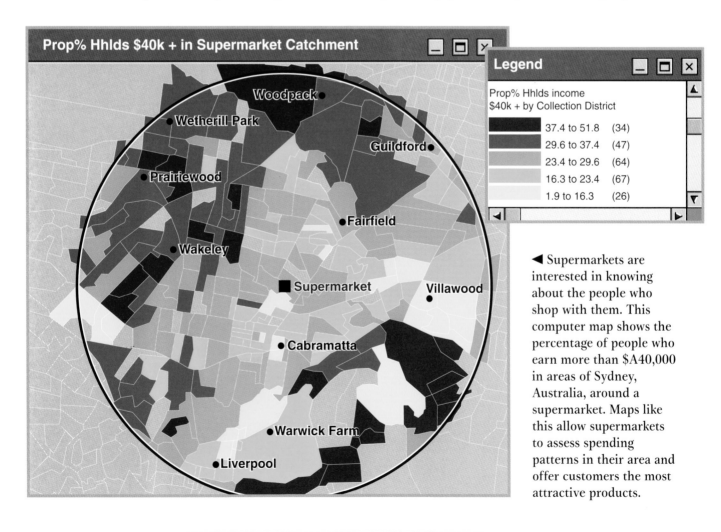

◀ Supermarkets are interested in knowing about the people who shop with them. This computer map shows the percentage of people who earn more than $A40,000 in areas of Sydney, Australia, around a supermarket. Maps like this allow supermarkets to assess spending patterns in their area and offer customers the most attractive products.

Election Mapping

A democracy is a form of government in which all of the adult people in a country have the right to vote in elections to decide who is to govern them. Countries such as the U.S., the U.K., Germany, France, Japan, Canada, and Russia are all democracies. Democratic governments use maps to draw up electoral districts.

In a democracy the country is divided into areas within which the population can vote for a person to represent them in the government. The electors vote for people who are usually members of a political party. A political party is a group of people who share political beliefs and aims, and who organize themselves in a way so as to achieve those aims through politics.

In the U.S. people living in each state not only vote for a president but also for someone to represent them in both the House of Representatives and the Senate. The number of Congressmen each state has to represent it in the House of Representatives depends on the population of that state. However, each state, whatever its population size, votes for two senators to represent it in the Senate. Each state is divided into districts, and

▼ The results of the U.S. presidential elections in 2000. The vote in Florida was very close and led to legal challenges to President Bush's overall victory.

Election 2000
States won, percent of votes won, electoral votes gained and voter turnout per state

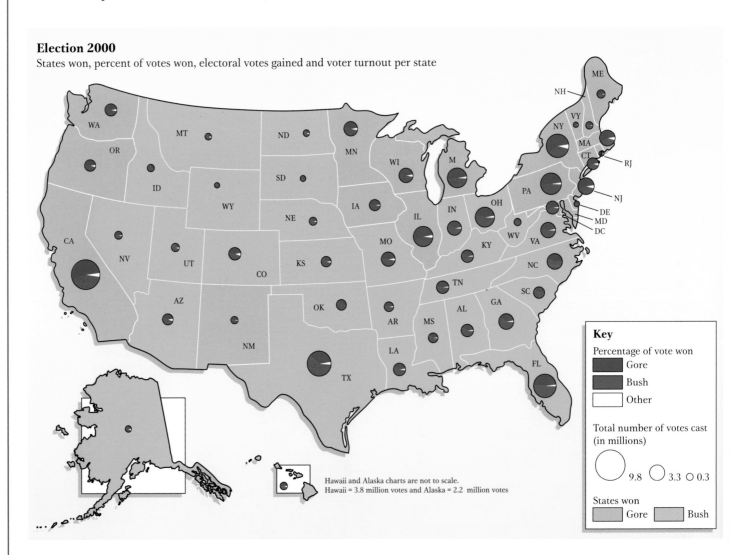

Hawaii and Alaska charts are not to scale.
Hawaii = 3.8 million votes and Alaska = 2.2 million votes

Key

Percentage of vote won
- Gore
- Bush
- Other

Total number of votes cast (in millions)
9.8   3.3   0.3

States won
- Gore
- Bush

SEE ALSO: *LAYERING INFORMATION* **2**: *10–11; MAPPING PEOPLE* **6**: *18–19*

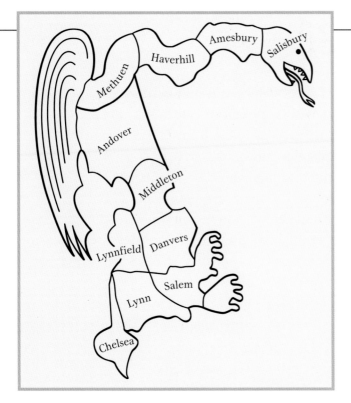

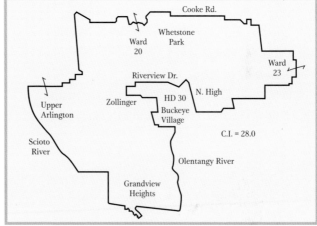

◀ A cartoon of Governor Gerry's drawing of district boundaries, showing them as a kind of monster. The trick in gerrymandering was to make sure that opposing voters were all lumped together in one district. They would get only one vote. Neighboring (pro-Gerry) districts with fewer people in them got the same.

▼ A "misshapen" electoral district in Franklin County, Ohio. The "hole" in the middle is an area of student housing for the Ohio State University. The students would tend to be Democrat voters, while the voters inside this district are predominantly Republicans.

here too elections take place to elect representatives to a wide range of roles within the state government. None of these electoral processes are possible without accurate maps. And the results make much more sense to the people with explanatory maps.

When and how an election takes place varies within a country and between countries. American presidents are elected for four years, while in France they are elected for six years.

There are many variations of democratic systems. In Italy, for example, there are two elected bodies, the Chamber of Deputies and the Senate. The people vote individually for representatives in each. They can vote for a a deputy when they are 18, but for a senator only when they are 25. This–along with the use of *proportional representation* and the existence of many political parties–makes mapping the results almost impossible.

Nowadays maps play an important part in the huge television coverage of elections in all countries. TV studios use graphics of all kinds to show the results as they come in and the patterns of voting that are emerging. Similar maps are found in newspapers the next day.

Using Maps to Cheat
People in certain areas of a country tend to favor certain political parties. When such differences in voting patterns and preferences have become known, some politicians have moved the boundaries between election districts in order to seek an advantage. Redrawing electoral districts to give one political party an unfair advantage is called gerrymandering. The name comes from Governor Elbridge Gerry of Massachusetts.

In 1812 a law was passed dividing the state into districts, each of which could vote for a state senator. The district boundaries were however drawn in such a way as to give the political advantage to Governor Gerry's own party, the Republicans. The outline of one of these districts on the map looked like a salamander, so combining this with the governor's name created the new word "gerrymander."

Wartime Maps

It almost seems as if war could not take place without maps, or at least not a modern war. Maps are essential to armies, navies, and air forces. They need to know where they are and where the enemy is. They need maps to help them prepare attacks and defend themselves. The capture of an enemy's map gives an army a great tactical advantage.

The importance of maps in wartime can be seen by the fact that more than 34 million maps of the Western Front in France and Belgium were produced by the British, French, and American Allies during World War I (1914–18) and almost as many by the Germans and other Central Powers.

During World War II British leader Winston Churchill used an underground bunker as the center of his operations rooms in London. They were known as the Cabinet War Rooms, and in them was a place called the Map Room. It was here that, using maps hanging on the walls, battles were planned, and the progress of the war was monitored. They included maps of the Atlantic Ocean and the position of warships in the seas around the U.K. and maps showing the progress of American forces as they invaded island after island in the Pacific.

More than 2,000 years before World War II the *lack* of a map probably stopped the conquest of India by the Greek commander Alexander the Great.

▼ Union General Quincy Gillmore studies a huge map of Charleston during the Civil War. Gillmore's Union troops were beseiging the city, which was being held by Confederate soldiers in 1863.

▲ U.S. Army trucks move supplies in preparation for the advance at Meuse-Argonne, France, in 1918. Maps showed the drivers that there was a road and that it was overlooked by German positions in the far hills.

▼ Millions of these trench maps were produced during World War I. This one was used in an attack at Meuse-Argonne (above) by the American Army 1st Division on October 9, 1918. It shows the objectives for the attack.

Having conquered the huge Persian Empire and entered India, his weary army would go no further and mutinied. They simply did not know what lay ahead of them, and–despite the surveyors who accompanied him into Asia–neither did Alexander. Military history is full of moments when maps, and the interpretation of maps, made a huge difference.

Deadly Mapping Errors

Wartime maps have to be accurate, and those who use them must know how to read them. Mistakes have frequently been made in wartime that have resulted in the loss of lives of both soldiers and

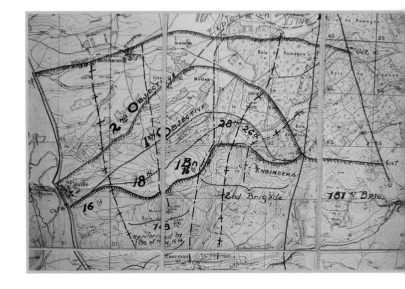

civilians. Artillery has hit and killed its own troops either because the map was wrongly drawn, *coordinates* were wrongly given or understood, or the map was out-of-date.

Appearances Can Be Deceptive

Some map-reading mistakes have cost an entire war. Distances can look much shorter on a map than they are in reality. Converting a circular globe into a flat map also distorts distances.

Some historians think that maps deceived the German leader in World War II, Adolf Hitler, into the mistake of invading the Soviet Union because Berlin does not look far from Moscow on a map. The huge distances involved and the long supply lines to his troops contributed toward his eventual defeat in both the Soviet Union and the war itself.

Mapping the Seabed

It was not the needs and desires of geologists or marine scientists that led to the mapping of the ocean beds. It was those of the military. Some modern navies have nuclear-powered submarines that can remain at sea for long periods of time.

Many have inter-continental ballistic missiles (ICBMs) that can carry a nuclear warhead.

These submarines need to hide from enemy hunter-killer submarines designed to find and destroy them in the event of a war. The need to find areas of the seabed on which to hide a nuclear submarine (and where to look for them) resulted in the mapping of the Atlantic and Arctic Ocean seabeds. This led to important discoveries about the movement of the earth's crust (*plate tectonics*).

▼ A U.S. soldier punching map coordinates into the targeting system on a multiple-launch rocket system.

▶ A digital map being used by students at the U.S. Army War College in Carlisle, Pennsylvania. The ability to read a map and understand the terrain forms an important part of their basic training. These digital maps are provided by the National Imagery and Mapping Agency. NIMA produces maps for the U.S. military.

Maps from Spies

On page 8 we saw that Louis XIV arranged for maps to be drawn of the French coastline and that he was not happy with the results. He also had maps drawn of fortresses around the borders and coasts of France. In addition, using spies, he had maps made of forts in other countries.

Security was very lax in the French king's court, and after the maps were created, copies of the maps were made. In 1683 the English ambassador in France contacted the English king Charles II and told him that he could get copies of the maps of French fortifications. The ambassador passed them on to Charles. They showed him more modern methods of building forts and castles.

More recently, many maps of different areas of the world have been prepared by the Central Intelligence Agency (CIA) for use by the U.S. military. They were made with modern methods of spying, using reconnaissance aircraft flying very high over enemy territory or with images from satellites. These maps provide accurate information not normally available about parts of the world.

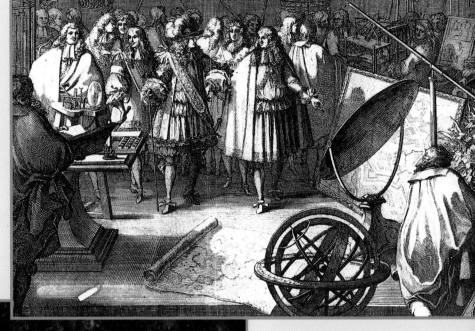

▲ Maps and a celestial globe feature in this engraving of Louis XIV, king of France, visiting the Academy of Sciences. The academy had been set up by him to study such topics as math and chemistry−but not espionage!

FISHBEDS WITH MISSILES UNDER WINGS

◄ A photograph taken from a U.S. spy plane during the 1962 Cuban Missile Crisis. Aerial photos like these become maps.

Propaganda Mapping

▲ Danti Ignazio's painting of the Battle of Lepanto in the Vatican map room. The Latin at the top of the map translates as "The Turkish Fleet Routed."

Propaganda is a way of altering people's attitudes, opinions, and views of another person or of an issue. It often involves telling lies or distorting the truth. Usually, propaganda is delivered through the written word, in speeches, or by an image. But maps can be a very effective way of putting over a message and altering a person's opinion. That is because people tend to trust a map. Maps seem to be *objective* rather than *subjective* illustrations. Because they are based on measurements of the world, they appear to tell the truth.

Using maps as propaganda is not new. Some of the earliest maps were drawn to show the amount of land a person owned. The maps were designed not just to record land ownership but also to make the person look really important and influential. They were a kind of propaganda.

In the Vatican in Rome is a map gallery called the *Galleria delle Carte Geografiche*. First decorated in 1580, this magnificent room has a painting on the ceiling and painted maps on the walls showing the towns, districts, and provinces of Italy. The purpose of the room was to show Italy's special place in the Christian world and the importance of the Pope. It also showed that the Pope was an important patron of the arts, with the money and influence to employ the most famous painters.

Among the maps in this room is one depicting the Battle of Lepanto (1571). A Turkish Islamic force was attempting to conquer the Mediterranean island of Cyprus. A fleet fitted out by by Pope Pius V, the city of Venice, and Philip II, king of Spain, defeated the Turkish force, capturing 117 galleys and thousands of prisoners. This Christian victory was not really significant because Venice surrendered Cyprus to the Turks two years later. But it was a great boost to the morale of Christians, who were losing influence and power in some areas to Islam. This map (right) is not a lie, but it is propaganda.

The North American "Map War"

In 1718 the French mapmaker Guillaume Delisle produced a map called *La Carte de la Louisiane et du Cours du Mississippi* (Map of Louisiana and the Course of the Mississippi River). He was paid by the French king for the work. On the map *La Louisiane* is placed in broad letters across the entire Louisiana basin, and the English colonies are squeezed into a small area on the eastern coast. This map was a form of propaganda. It claimed a huge area of land for France to the west of the Appalachians.

It quickly provoked a response from the British. In 1720 Hermann Moll, a German map publisher working in London, produced "This Map of North America According to ye Newest and most Exact Observations." On this map the British colonies stretch from the Carolinas to Newfoundland, and the ocean off the eastern seaboard is marked as "Sea of the British Empire." Several more maps were created by the French and the British in the following decades, each one laying claim to North American land. Each was a piece of propaganda, with no real basis in reality. Neither the French nor the British actually controlled the vast tracts of land claimed at the time the maps were produced.

Propaganda as Preparation for War

When World War I ended in 1918, Germany lost much of its territory. German mapmakers started producing maps designed to show the country as badly treated and under threat. These maps skillfully used colors and symbols, with Germany always shown surrounded by powerful enemies.

The perceptions these maps helped create in Germany contributed to the rise to power of the Nazis. When they took over in 1933, they continued to make these maps, preparing the German people for war.

► Nothing is different on these two maps except the shading. But map **(a)** seems to be "unstable," the "weight" of countries presses on South Africa. Map **(b)** seems less threatening. Even something as simple as shading or color can change the way the map reader interprets a map. Although they may look like scientific facts, maps can argue a point of view, which means they can be used as propaganda.

▼ A German propaganda map from the 1930s, "A SMALL STATE THREATENS GERMANY." Bomber aircraft from Czechoslovakia can apparently reach all of Germany. But the Czechs had no bomber aircraft!

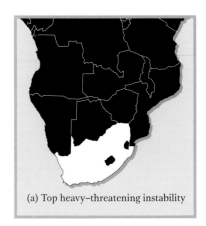

(a) Top heavy–threatening instability

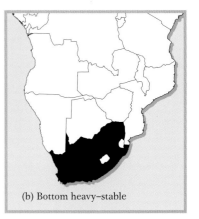

(b) Bottom heavy–stable

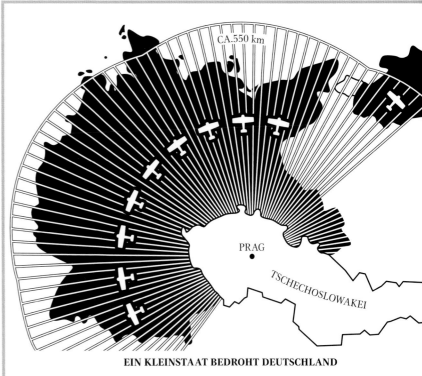

CA.550 km

PRAG

TSCHECHOSLOWAKEI

EIN KLEINSTAAT BEDROHT DEUTSCHLAND

Mapping the Enemy

The need for up-to-date, accurate maps is essential during a war, but drawing maps of an enemy's territory is very difficult. The enemy is not too eager to be mapped! Often old maps have to be relied on to form the basis of new ones.

During World War I trench maps were based on prewar French maps that were updated in several daring ways. Maps of areas behind enemy lines were often drawn from observation balloons and aircraft. Soldiers used to go on trench raids at night across no-man's land. The aim was to capture prisoners who were then interrogated for information. In some cases the prisoners had maps that showed which troops were where. While out on these raids the soldiers also drew maps of the enemy trenches.

During World War II the maps used by the military were based on very old tourist maps of countries, produced by commercial map-publishing firms. In preparing for the Falklands War (1982) and the Gulf War (1991) the British Army had to appeal to the general public for any old maps or books of both areas.

In both world wars reconnaissance aircraft flew over enemy territory taking photographs of the land below. During World War II aircraft such as the Spitfire, the P-51 Mustang, and the Mosquito flew at both high and low altitude over Nazi-occupied Europe. They took photographs that were used to

▼ Shot-down U-2 spy planes on display in Tianamen Square, Beijing. They had been taking spy photographs over China that could have been used for mapping.

SEE ALSO: *MEASURING FROM PHOTOGRAPHS* **2**: *22–25*; *RASTER IMAGES FROM SPACE* **8**: *18–23*

◀ ▼ Just a few days after the first manned hot-air balloon flight by the French Montgolfier brothers in 1783 a French journalist wrote, "I am convinced this apparatus could be very useful to an army for discovering the positions of its enemy." He was right. Balloons were used in all wars for surveillance of the enemy up to and including World War I (left). The 1964 SR-71 (below) did the same job—but at a height of 15 miles and at 2,220 mph (3,550 km/h)!

locate enemy troops and buildings of importance such as armament factories. They were also used as the basis for producing accurate, up-to-date maps for use in the invasion of Europe. Maps of the invasion beaches in Normandy in 1944 were drawn using aerial photographs and even old postcards.

Flights of this kind do not take place only in wartime. The Germans flew civil airliners over Britain in the 1930s before World War II in order to take photographs. At the same time, the Germans were buying Ordnance Survey maps of the country.

On these maps military information such as the location of airfields, gun batteries, and radar stations was deliberately missing. But the Germans were able to use their aerial photographs to alter and update the maps they had bought.

Misleading Maps

Using the enemy's maps can be misleading. Not only are important features such as airports often missing, but also the enemy can deliberately put things in the wrong place. During the 1930s, and especially during the Cold War of the 1960s, Soviet mapmakers deliberately put topographical information such as towns, rivers, hills, and coastlines in the wrong place on maps and atlases sold to the public.

In order to make more accurate maps and to gather information, reconnaissance flights also took place during the Cold War. In 1962 an American U-2 aircraft flown by a pilot called Gary Powers was shot down over what was then the Soviet Union. It was

on a spying mission and taking photographs that could have been used to map the land. The U-2 was able to fly very high but did not fly very fast. It was replaced by the SR-71, which can fly at at a height of 24,000 meters (80,000 ft) at a speed of Mach 3.

In the last three decades satellites, which can be used to map enemy territory, have reduced the need for reconnaissance flights. They orbit around the earth and can take very detailed photographs of the land below. The maps drawn from them can be produced very quickly.

Command, Control, Communication

For any war to be won, a military leader must be able to command and control his troops. To do this, he must be able to communicate with them and gather information about the enemy. To win a modern war, electronic command and control systems are essential.

Military Mapmakers

The job of producing maps for the U.S. military is in the hands of the National Imagery and Mapping Agency (NIMA), which was set up in 1996. It uses information from satellites, aircraft, and other sources to produce up-to-date and accurate images,

Eye in the Sky

Those countries that are members of the North Atlantic Treaty Organisation (NATO), such as the U.S., Canada, and the U.K., use aircraft like the Boeing A-3 Sentry to get information. This airplane, which is also known as AWACS (Airborne Warning and Control System), has a huge radar dome on its back, which is able to look down on a large area and spot movement of enemy aircraft, ships, and vehicles.

These movements are shown on radar displays that resemble video-game screens. Large crews of radar operators use the radar to detect the speed and positions of targets, which are overlaid onto topographic maps showing roads, towns, rivers, hills, and other prominent features. They use these electronic maps to control and direct their own forces against the enemy and to spot any attacks.

The high-resolution radar on these aircraft can produce three-dimensional images that show the shape of the land in great detail. Satellites can also produce detailed maps of the surface of the earth, and from them accurate topographical maps can be made.

As a result, producing up-to-date maps of any area of the world can be done quickly and accurately without having to use old, out-of-date maps or spies on the ground.

▼ The Boeing A-3 Sentry can provide "real time" data to ground troops and other aircraft.

SEE ALSO: *WARTIME MAPS* **6:** *22–25; VIRTUAL ENVIRONMENTS* **8:** *34–35*

intelligence, and geospatial information in the form of maps to support the U.S. military. NIMA produces maps for evasion and the location of targets for cruise missiles and bomber aircraft, and is also able to display on a computer screen a three-dimensional view of an area of land showing the shape of the earth. Soldiers can now sit at a computer and see a 3-D image of anywhere in the world they maybe asked to fight.

These high-resolution radar maps are used to program cruise missiles such as the Tomahawk. This missile guides itself to its target following a map of its intended route that has been made using radar images from satellites and aircraft. The map is programmed into the Tomahawk's guidance system before launch. On its way to the target it uses its own radar to check the route it is following against the route that has been fed in, and it also checks on its position using a satellite global positioning system (GPS) in its guidance system. This missile was used during the Gulf War, on targets in Serbia and Iraq since then, and in Afghanistan.

At battlefield level pilotless aircraft called RPVs (Remote Pilotless Vehicles) can fly over a battlefield and take photographs and gather information for making maps. These RPVs avoid having a valuable aircraft and its even more valuable human crew shot down and lost.

The electronic control system of modern armies is called C³I, which stands for Command, Control, Communication, and Information.

▲ A U.S. officer points to a map of Iraq in 1991 during the Gulf War. Iraq had invaded its neighbor, the country of Kuwait. A force dominated by the U.S. but including many other countries eventually freed Kuwait. At first maps like this were out-of-date, but satellite and aerial reconnaissance quickly improved them.

◄ This sketch map is a good example of how important information about his own troop positions has always been to a commander. The Union General Sherman demanded that corps engineers in his army during the Civil War send him a map like this of their position at the end of *every day's* march. This map shows the position of the 15th Army Corps on February 16, 1865, in South Carolina.

Escape Maps

During World War II (1939–45) American, Russian, Japanese, German, Italian, and British aircrew were given maps that they could use to help them escape if they were shot down. The maps were part of an escape pack that included compasses concealed in buttons on their uniforms. The maps were small-scale, showing large areas.

The Allies' maps were made by the makers of the game Monopoly, using silk, rayon, or tissue paper. The maps were hidden in places such as the heel of a flying boot or in a cigarette case.

The mapmaking company was also involved in smuggling maps to prisoners of war held in Germany. They hid maps inside Monopoly boards, chess sets, and packs of playing cards, which were sent to prisoner-of-war camps.

In total more than 35,000 American, British, and other Allied prisoners escaped from behind enemy lines, and it is estimated that half of them had a silk map with them.

Often the prisoners in the camps made maps for themselves to help them escape. Philip Evans and Wallis Heath were both held in a prisoner-of-war camp outside Brunswick in Germany. They set up a printing press using the advice and guidance of other prisoners who were artists, chemists, and carpenters. Copying the silk maps that had been brought inside the camp, they used wall tiles as printing plates and pitch from between the floorboards as the basis for the ink. The men were eventually discovered and punished by being put into solitary confinement, but only after they had produced 500 copies of four different maps.

The National Imagery and Mapping Agency in the U.S. produces maps for use by the armed forces. Among the maps they make are so-called evasion maps, which are issued to U.S. pilots. In 1995 an Air Force officer named Captain Scott O'Grady was shot down over Bosnia. He managed to avoid being captured by the Serbian forces by using his evasion map. It not only helped him find his way out, but also gave him information about the area he was in and what he could or could not eat. Because it was waterproof, he could also use it to keep himself dry, use it as a groundsheet or tent—and even to carry water or food.

► A European escape and evasion map printed on cloth and issued to Allied soldiers and airmen in 1943. The map warns that "Owing to frontiers being constantly changed in Eastern Europe, those marked on the map must be accepted with reserve."

◄ This silk map for British pilots was also first produced in 1943. But in 1953 it was updated for the *Cold War* (see glossary). Useful words were provided in Czech and Romanian.

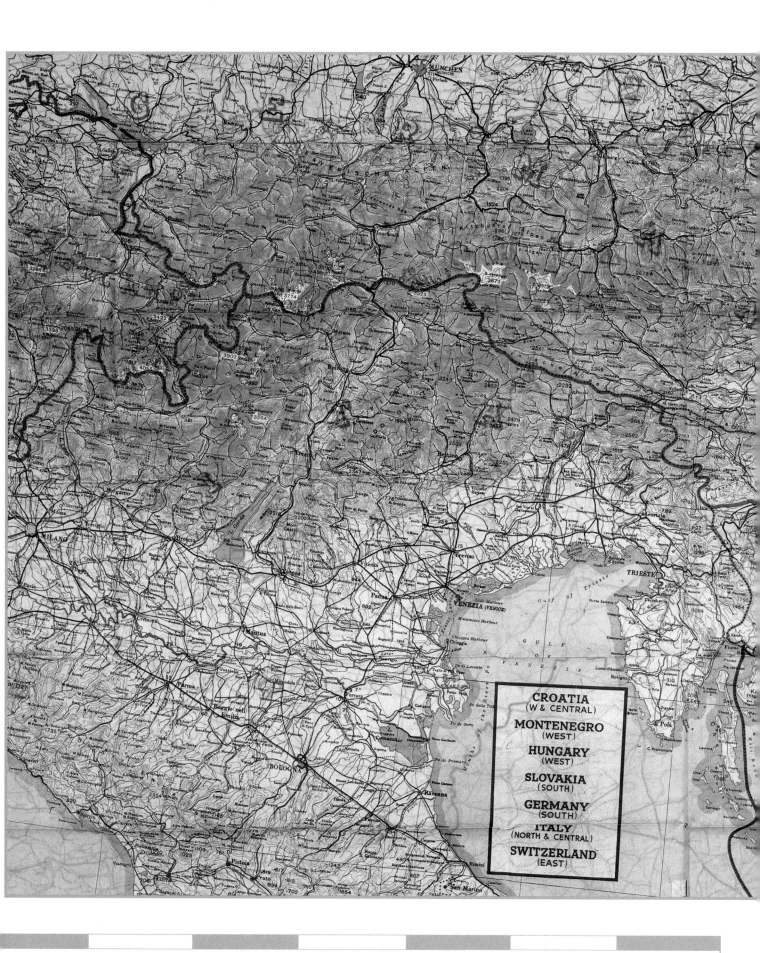

CROATIA
(W & CENTRAL)
MONTENEGRO
(WEST)
HUNGARY
(WEST)
SLOVAKIA
(SOUTH)
GERMANY
(SOUTH)
ITALY
(NORTH & CENTRAL)
SWITZERLAND
(EAST)

Mapping for International Agencies

The United Nations is an organization that was set up in October 1945 at the end of World War II to try to preserve peace and avoid any future wars. Originally, the UN had 51 members, but that has now increased to 189, nearly all the nations of the world. Today the UN does not just send peacekeeping troops to world troublespots; it has many departments involved in attempting to improve human society in various ways. All these departments use maps, which the UN often creates for itself.

In 1944, toward the end of World War II, in an area of southern Europe known as the Balkans a new country was created called Yugoslavia. It was formed from six smaller countries called Bosnia-Herzegovina, Croatia, Macedonia, Montenegro, Serbia, and Slovenia. In each of them, however, different religious and ethnic groups existed, and for centuries there has been conflict between them.

From 1944 until his death in 1980 Josip Broz Tito ruled Yugoslavia. He was a communist dictator who ruled this new country by force and persuasion. After his death Yugoslavia became unstable, and the jealousies and friction that existed between its republics broke out into armed conflicts after 1981.

In April 1992 civil war broke out in Bosnia-Herzegovina, where two groups of people, Serbs and Bosnians, were living together. The Republic of Serbia, aided by the Bosnian-Serbs, tried to take land from Bosnia to make Serbia larger. The Serbs cleared any non-Serbian people from an area of Bosnia in a terrible military operation that became known as ethnic cleansing. Eventually, the United Nations arrived as peacekeepers.

Only after NATO air attacks and military defeats by a Bosnian Army equipped and trained by the U.S. did the Serbs agree to peace talks. They took

▲ The Central Intelligence Agency (CIA) has an extensive library of maps it has drawn of any area of the world where the U.S. may become involved. This is one of their maps of the area that used to make up the country of Yugoslavia.

place in Dayton, Ohio. In November 1995 the Dayton Peace Agreement was signed.

An important part of the peace agreement was the maps of the area drawn by the then Defense Mapping Agency (it was to become part of the National Imagery and Mapping Agency in 1996). They were drawn to enable the peace delegates of the two sides to see who was to get what in terms of land and resources. They were able to see a three-dimensional picture of the land they were disputing. Four million dollar's-worth of high-tech equipment and 55 mapping personnel worked to help in the success of the negotiations.

SEE ALSO: THE SCRAMBLE FOR AFRICA 5: 28–31

But just because a map has been drawn, that does not mean that borders are accepted by everyone. The map (left), for example, has a note saying, "Serbia and Montenegro have asserted the formation of a joint independent state, but this entity has not been formally recognized as a state by the United States." The U.S. is questioning this new, larger nation. Did the governments of the two states have the support of their peoples for this redrawing of the map?

A similar civil war took place in the Balkans during 1999 in Kosovo. There, as in Bosnia, when the conflicts were settled, the many minefields laid became a major problem, killing many innocent people who were eager to go back to their homes. There are still more than a million mines in Bosnia.

▲ A CIA map of Kosovo. In 1999 a civil war there ended only after intervention by the U.S. and its allies. After many weeks of bombing, Serbian forces withdrew from Kosovo prior to a NATO invasion from Macedonia.

▼ A world map showing where landmines have been planted in astonishing numbers. Many of them are in countries where the conflict is over, but the countries do not have the financial or technical means to clear them.

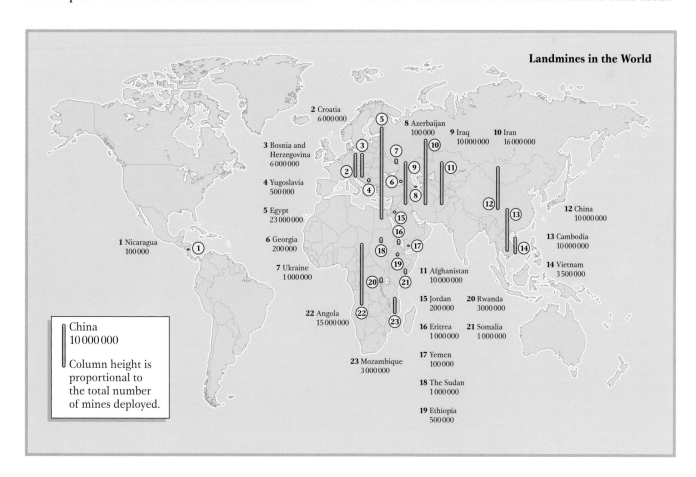

Landmines in the World

2 Croatia 6 000 000
3 Bosnia and Herzegovina 6 000 000
4 Yugoslavia 500 000
5 Egypt 23 000 000
6 Georgia 200 000
7 Ukraine 1 000 000
8 Azerbaijan 100 000
9 Iraq 10 000 000
10 Iran 16 000 000
11 Afghanistan 10 000 000
12 China 10 000 000
13 Cambodia 10 000 000
14 Vietnam 3 500 000
15 Jordan 200 000
16 Eritrea 1 000 000
17 Yemen 100 000
18 The Sudan 1 000 000
19 Ethiopia 500 000
20 Rwanda 3 000 000
21 Somalia 1 000 000
22 Angola 15 000 000
23 Mozambique 3 000 000
1 Nicaragua 100 000

China 10 000 000
Column height is proportional to the total number of mines deployed.

Many millions of mines have been laid throughout the world in other areas. Accidents from land mines are as common as road accidents.

Often the location of the mines is unknown because no maps were ever drawn. The lack of a map can be deliberate, but it can also be due to the lack of time to draw one when laying the mines. Sometimes the map is deliberately drawn incorrectly to trick the enemy.

Other Areas of Conflict

The United Nations is involved in peacekeeping operations throughout the world: in Europe in Bosnia, Kosovo, and Croatia, in Africa in places such as Sierra Leone and Ethiopia, in Asia in places like East Timor, and in the Middle East. More than 38,000 troops, all wearing their distinctive blue helmets or berets and sometimes backed up by police forces, try to keep enemies apart and build trust between them. It is difficult and sometimes deadly work.

▼ A United Nations peacekeeper wearing his light blue helmet. His vehicle has been painted white to show it belongs to the UN. But the UN is not just a peacekeeping army: it supervises, for example, the World Health Organization.

▶ A map made by UN High Commissioner for Refugees in 1999 showing the location of refugee camps in the Middle East. The large number of camps in Pakistan held refugees who had already fled from the Taliban regime in Afghanistan.

▶ When a civil war breaks out in a country, many people leave it in the hope of finding safety in neighboring countries. These people are called refugees. Some have no choice but to leave their homes, forced from them by their enemies, as happened to Bosnians in 1992. This photograph shows a Bosnian refugee camp in 1995 in which the people have to live in tents.

SEE ALSO: "GOOD FENCES MAKE GOOD NEIGHBORS" 5: 32–35

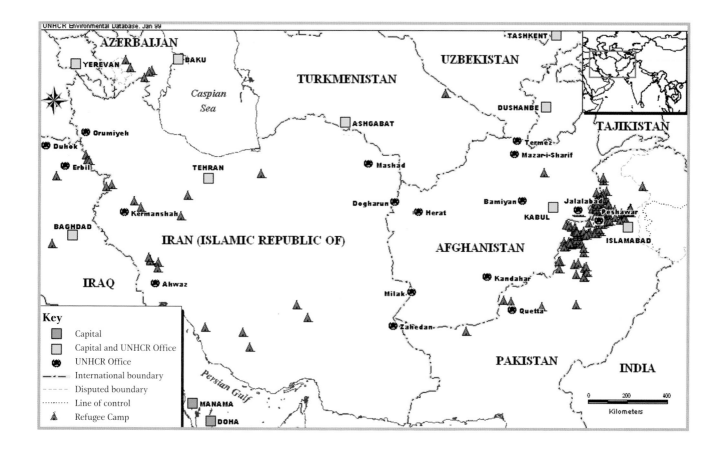

Key
- Capital
- Capital and UNHCR Office
- UNHCR Office
- — - — International boundary
- - - - - Disputed boundary
- .... Line of control
- Refugee Camp

An "Umbrella" Organization

In these areas other United Nations agencies also work, including the UN High Commissioner for Refugees, the World Food Program, and the United Nations Children's Fund (UNICEF).

The UN attempts to work toward improvements in various aspects of life across the globe, such as the defense of human rights, protection for the environment, and the fight against disease and poverty. It does this through more than 30 organizations, including the World Bank, the International Monetary Fund (IMF), the United Nations Educational, Scientific, and Cultural Organization (UNESCO), the International Court of Justice, and the World Health Organization (WHO).

The WHO is sometimes criticized for attempting to solve problems in poorer countries by using Western drugs. This can look like a way of boosting the profits of Western drugs companies, rather than tackling the underlying reasons for disease, which can be poor sanitation or nutrition.

In all of its operations the UN sees a great demand for maps. Its own cartographic section provides them. It produces general maps of more than 100 countries as well as peacekeeping maps showing where UN peacekeepers are being used.

In addition the UN has a huge collection of some 80,000 maps, as well as more than 3,000 atlases, *gazetteers*, travel guides, and cartographic reference works. This library is part of the Dag Hammarskjold Library at the UN Headquarters in New York.

Among the reference books are some dealing with international boundaries. Some are published by the International Boundary Research Unit based at the University of Durham in England. This organization seeks to gather information to allow border disputes between countries to be resolved peacefully. It is the only research center of its kind in the world.

Glossary

Words in *italics* have their own entries in the glossary

Académie des Sciences (Academy of Sciences) – first established in 1666 as the Académie Royale des Sciences, a small, elite French society in which the most prominent scientific people of the time gathered to advance the progress of science

Aerial photograph (or air photograph) – a photograph looking straight down at the earth, taken from an airplane

Alexander the Great (356–323 B.C.) – Alexander succeeded his father Philip II as king of Macedon (an ancient Greek state). Alexander was one of the greatest generals of all time, who conquered much of Asia and the Middle East and influenced the spread of Greek culture

Astronomy – the scientific study of celestial bodies (planets and stars) and of the universe as a whole. People who do this are called astronomers

"Bonnie Prince Charlie" (1720–1788) – Charles Edward Stuart, who claimed the English throne and led the unsuccessful Jacobite Rebellion of 1745–46 in Scotland. His grandfather was the exiled Roman Catholic King James II, who had ruled from 1685 to 1688

Atlas – a collection of maps with a uniform design bound together as a book

Cadastral system – a method of recording ownership of land based on registers, legal docu-ments, and maps showing the boundaries of individual tracts

Cartographer – someone who collects information and produces maps from it; the task of making maps is called cartography

Cartouche – originally a cartouche was a list of royal or divine names on an ancient Egyptian scroll. Later, map cartouches were elaborate decorations with dedications inside them, naming the sponsors of the map (often royalty). Today the cartouche often contains the map title, *legend*, and *scale*

Census – a detailed count, usually taken every ten years, of how many people there are in a country, plus details about their lives

Central Powers – during World War I Germany and Austria-Hungary and their allies Turkey and Bulgaria

Churchill, Sir Winston (1874–1965) – prime minister who led Britain during World War II from 1940 to 1945; a statesman, soldier, and author

Cold War – the relationship that existed between the U.S. (and its allies) and the former USSR (and its allies) from the end of World War II to about 1990; both groups kept large numbers of troops and weapons in the event of the other side attacking them

Colony – a group of people who settle in a land distant from their homeland but retain close economic and cultural links with it; the territory they inhabit and control

Coordinates – the pair of values that define a position on a graph or on a map with a coordinate system (such as latitude and longitude). On a map the coordinates "55ºN 45ºE" indicate a position of 55 degrees north of latitude, 45 degrees east of longitude

Cruise missile – an unmanned rocket that, when launched from a ship or submarine, can navigate to its target by skimming low over the surface, avoiding enemy radar and matching the picture of the ground with the preprogrammed map of the route to the eventual target

Cuban missile crisis – in 1962 the USSR began shipping nuclear missiles into Cuba. Once U-2 spy planes had spotted the missiles, the U.S. blockaded the island to stop the missile shipments. After a tense week with both sides preparing for war, the Soviet premier Nikita Khrushchev withdrew the missiles

Democracy – a form of government in which all of the adult people in a country have the right to vote in elections to decide who is to govern them

Demographic map – a map showing details of the human population; such maps often rely on *census* information

Ecosystem – the relationship between living things and with their environment; zebras, lions, and African grassland are all part of the same ecosystem

Engraving – the art of inscribing a design onto a block, plate, or other surface used for printing

Ethnic cleansing – the removal of people of a different color, religion, or ethnic background to that of the dominant group from an area through force or intim-idation–sometimes murder

Gazetteer – a list of names of places, with their location specified; often accompanied by a map

Geology – the study of the rocks under the earth's surface and their structure

Geological maps – maps that show the structure of the rocks underneath an area

Geospatial information – information about where things are on the earth's surface and what their characteristics are

Gerrymandering – the process of manipulating voting districts in order to distort the results of elections

Global Positioning System (GPS) – a system of 24 man-made satellites orbiting the earth and sending out highly accurate radio signals indicating where they are; a GPS receiver held by someone on the earth can interpret the signals and calculate the receiver's position on earth

Grid system – a reference system that uses a mesh of horizontal and vertical lines over the face of a map to pinpoint the position of places. The mesh of lines often helps show distance of locations east and north from a set position. The zero point can be any convenient location and is often the bottom-left corner of the map

Infrastructure – the public facilities built up over a number of years that are used by people in their daily lives. Examples include the transportation system, power supply, and sewerage system

Internet – the network of interconnected computers throughout the world linked by wires and satellites and running software to allow them to communicate with each other

Land mines – explosive devices usually buried just under the surface of the ground and sensitive to humans walking or driving over them; they are used to target enemy soldiers, but after military action has finished, they are a major danger to civilians

Land use – how human beings use land, for example, for housing, agriculture, or recreation. Land use is different from land cover, which describes the natural vegetation or environment in an area, for example, forest, desert, or ice cap

Legend – a list of all the symbols used on a map with an explanation of their meaning

Mach speed – a measure of speed compared to the speed of sound; Mach 1 is equivalent to about 750 miles per hour, which is the speed of sound

Mercator, Gerardus (1512–1594) – a cartographer, born in Antwerp

(present-day Belgium), who created new designs for maps, developed the concept of the atlas, and devised a famous map projection very useful for navigators

Nazi – member of the National Socialist German Worker's Party that seized control of Germany in 1933 under Adolf Hitler

North Atlantic Treaty Organization (NATO) – a group of countries in Europe and North America that have agreed to work together to defend themselves in the event of one or more of them being attacked

National Imagery and Mapping Agency (NIMA) – an organization that produces maps and other geographic information for the American military

National mapping agency – a government-run organization responsible for producing mainly *topographic maps* of an entire country

Objective and subjective – if someone has an objective view of a subject, they are reacting only to the facts, without letting their emotions or prejudices affect their judgement. But a subjective opinion is personal and does not rely only on the facts. *Propaganda* appeals to subjective emotions

Ordnance Survey – the national mapping agency of Great Britain

Photogrammetry – the science of making accurate measurements from photographs of the world

Plate tectonics – the study of the movements of the plates or sections that make up the earth's crust. These plates ride on the semimolten rock inside the crust

Propaganda – a way of altering the attitudes, opinions, and views of another person about an issue by producing written documents or graphical materials such as maps or through the spoken word

Proportional representation – a *democratic* system of voting based on the principle that voters should have representatives in government in proportion to their share of the overall vote. This allows voters in a minority to win their fair share of representation

Prospectus – an invitation to become involved with some kind of commercial scheme

Radar – a method of detecting distant objects by bouncing high-frequency radio waves off them and interpreting the return signal

Reconnaissance – for the military the task of obtaining information about the land and the enemy's position

Relief – the shape of the earth's surface, its hills, mountains, and depressions

San Andreas Fault – a major fault in the earth's crust in Southern California, where earthquake risk is high; the disastrous San Francisco earthquake of 1906 was caused by movement along the fault (*see also* Plate tectonics)

Scale – the ratio of the size of a map to the area of the real world that it represents

Seismic survey – using explosives to set off small earth tremors. Interpretation of the results reveals information about the structure of the rocks beneath

Surveying – the measuring of altitudes, angles, and distances on the land surface in order to obtain accurate positions of features that can be mapped. Surveying the oceans and seas also means measuring distances and angles between visible coastal positions, but the third dimension measured is depth rather than height

Theodolite – a surveying instrument used to figure out the angle between two points on the earth's surface viewed from a third point

Topographic map – a map that shows natural features such as hills, rivers, and forests, and man-made features such as roads and buildings

Triangulation – a surveying method, using angles alone to figure out the position of points on the earth's surface

United Nations – an organization set up in October 1945 at the end of World War II in order to try to preserve peace and avoid future wars; almost every country in the world now belongs to the UN

United States Geological Survey – the national mapping agency of the U.S. It also undertakes scientific work in other fields such as geology and environmental sciences

Further Reading and Websites

Barber, Peter, ed. *The Lie of the Land*, British Library Publishing, 2001

Driver, Cline *Early American Maps and Views*, University Press of Virginia, 1988

Forte, I., et al., *Map Skills and Geography: Inventive Exercises to Sharpen Skills and Raise Achievement*, Incentive Publications, 1998

Haywood, John, et al., *Atlas of World History*, Barnes & Noble Books, 2001

Letham, Lawrence *GPS Made Easy*, Rocky Mountain Books, 1998

Monmonier, Mark *How to Lie with Maps*, University of Chicago Press, 1991

Monmonier, Mark *Map Appreciation*, Prentice Hall, 1988

Meltzer, M. *Columbus and the World around Him*, Franklin Watts, 1990

Stefoff, Rebecca *Young Oxford Companion to Maps and Mapmaking*, Oxford University Press, 1995

Thrower, Norman J. W. *Maps and Civilization: Cartography in Culture and Society*, 2nd ed., University of Chicago Press, 1999

Wilford, John. N. *The Mapmakers*, Pimlico, 2002

www.auslig.gov.au/
National mapping division of Australia. Find an aerial photograph of any area of the country

http://cgdi.gc.ca/ccatlas/atlas.htm
Internet-based Canadian Communities Atlas project. Schools create their own atlas

www.earthamaps.com/
Search by place name for U.S. city maps, with zoom facility

http://earthtrends.wri.org
World Resources Institute mapping of energy resources, agriculture, forestry, government, climate, and other thematic maps

http://geography.about.com
Links to pages on cartography, historic maps, GIS, and GPS; print out blank and outline maps for study purposes

http://ihr.sas.ac.uk/maps/
History of cartography; no images, but search for links to many other cartographic topics

www.lib.utexas.edu/maps/
Vast map collection at the University of Texas, historical and modern, including maps produced by the CIA

www.lib.virginia.edu/exhibits/lewis_clark/
Information on historic expeditions, including Lewis and Clark

www.lindahall.org/pubserv/hos/stars/
Exhibition of the Golden Age of the celestial atlas, 1482–1851

www.LivGenMI.com/1895.htm
A U.S. atlas first printed in 1895. Search for your town, city, or county

http://memory.loc.gov/ammem/gmdhtml/
Map collections 1500–1999, the Library of Congress; U.S. maps, including military campaigns and exploration

www.nationalgeographic.com/education/maps_geography/
The National Geographic educational site

http://oddens.geog.uu.nl/index.html
15,500 cartographic links; search by country or keyword

www.ordsvy.gov.uk/
Site of one of the oldest national mapping agencies. Search for and download historical and modern mapping of the U.K. Go to Understand Mapping page for cartographic glossary

www.mapzone.co.uk/
Competitions and quizzes for younger readers about Great Britain; site run by Ordnance Survey

http://www.libs.uga.edu/darchive/hargrett/maps/maps.html
University of Georgia historical map collection; maps from the 16th to the early 20th century

http://topozone.com/
Search by place name or latitude and longitude for all areas of the U.S. Maps at various scales

www.un.org/Depts/Cartographic/english/htmain.htm
United Nations cartographic section. Search by country and by different UN missions worldwide

http://mapping.usgs.gov/
U.S. national atlas and much more, including satellite images

http://interactive2.usgs.gov/learningweb/students/homework_geography.asp
USGS site for students; all kinds of useful information. Create your own map by plotting latitude and longitude coordinates

www.worldatlas.com/
World atlas and lots of statistics about all countries of the world

Set Index

Picture Credits

Abbreviation: C   Corbis

Jacket images Oblique view of antique map (background), Ken Reid/Telegraph Colour Library/Getty Images; T-in-O map of the world drawn in 1450 (inset, top), AKG London; three-dimensional map of the topography of Mars (inset, bottom), NASA/Science Photo Library. **6** Drukkerij Wormgoor b.v.; **7** Library of Congress; **8** Institut Géographique Nationale, Paris; **9** Bettmann/C; **10, 11** Reproduced from the Ordnance Survey map with the permission of Her Majesty's Stationery Office, © Crown Copyright, NC/01/23460 (Ordnance Survey holds an extensive archive of historical mapping and black and white copies on high quality paper or film are available, see website); **12l** U.S. Geological Survey; **12r** Roger Ressmeyer/C; **13** Maps of the National Topographic System of Canada; **15t, 15b** National Atlas of the U.S.A./Library of Congress; **16** Margaret S. Watters; **17** The Geological Society of London; **18** Hulton-Deutsch Collection/C; **19** Australian Bureau of Statistics; **22** C; **23t, 23b** M.F. Marix Evans; **24t** Nina Berman/Sipa Press/Rex Features; **24b** Leif Skoogfors/C; **25t** Harlingue-Viollet; **25b** Paul Crickmore; **26** Scala Group S.p.A; **28** Paul Crickmore; **29t** C; **29b** Lockheed Martin Corporation; **30** Bettmann/C; **31l** Gilder Lehrman Collection, on deposit at the Pierpont Morgan Library, N.Y.; **31r** David & Peter Turnley/C; **32** Andromeda Oxford Limited; **33** The British Library; **34, 35** Perry-Castañeda Library Map Collection/U.S. Central Intelligence Agency; **36t** Chris Rainier/C; **36b** David & Peter Turnley/C; **37** United Nations Cartographic Division.

While every effort has been made to trace the copyright holders of illustrations reproduced in this book, the publishers will be pleased to rectify any omissions or inaccuracies.